Part 2A Duets for Teacher and Student

In Memory of Frances Clark

By Ted Cooper
and
Amy Glennon

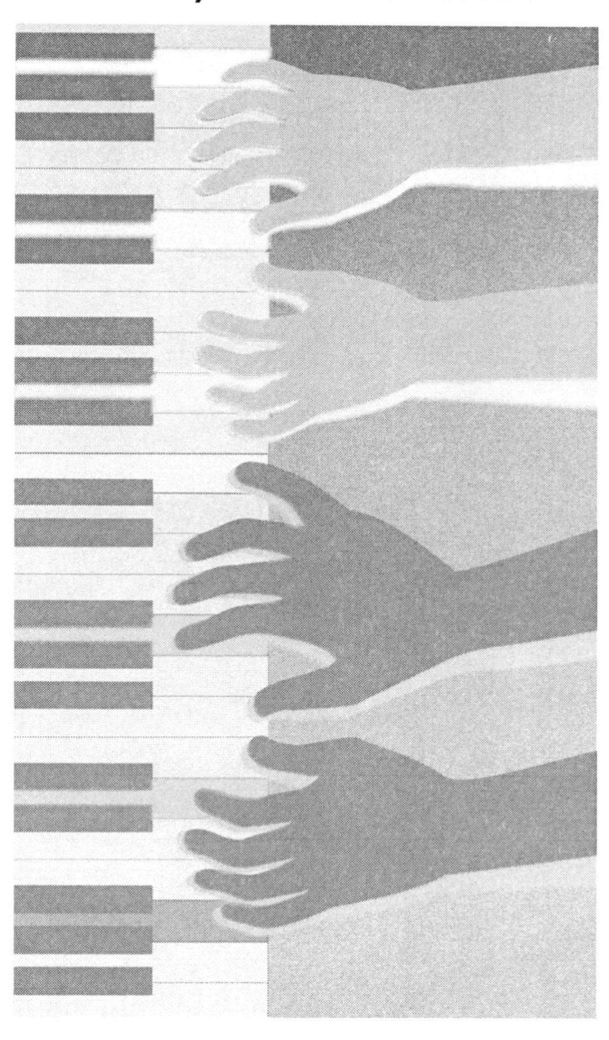

Summy-Birchard Inc., exclusively distributed by
Alfred Publishing Co., Inc.

Preface

There is nothing more exciting than a young pianist fully expressing a musical idea. The goal of this collection is to provide repertoire that encourages expressive playing using the natural capabilities of the elementary student. Because finding that perfect piece is central to a student's success and motivation, we have included a wide variety of styles—programmatic music, impressionistic music, blues, and traditional melodies. Although designed as duets, the student parts are satisfying when played as solos.

Side by Side Part 2A, coordinates with **Music Tree Part 2A**, of the *Frances Clark Library* but can be used with any method. For **Music Tree** teachers, we have grouped the pieces according to the unit in which they can first be taught. The pieces within each group have been listed in order of difficulty.

Unit 1	Unit 3	Unit 6	Unit 8
	Blocked 5ths	**New Landmarks**	
Brother John A Gentle Breeze The Wild West	Inside the Pyramid The Matador	Rodeo Homework Blues Cathedral Bells Snowy Day	Above the Clouds All the World Is Sleeping Scarborough Fair

We express our deep appreciation to Louise Goss, who has shaped our lives both in and out of the studio and whose tireless search for excellence is a daily inspiration.

We also wish to thank our colleagues at the Frances Clark Center for Keyboard Pedagogy, as well as the faculty and students at the New School for Music Study in Kingston, New Jersey, who tested pilot editions of this collection. We are especially grateful to Yat-Yee Chong, Scott Donald, Tracy Grandy, Alison Lont, Nancy Merkel, and Margaret Nelson for their valuable suggestions and support.

—Ted Cooper and Amy Glennon

Contents

The Wild West

Teacher

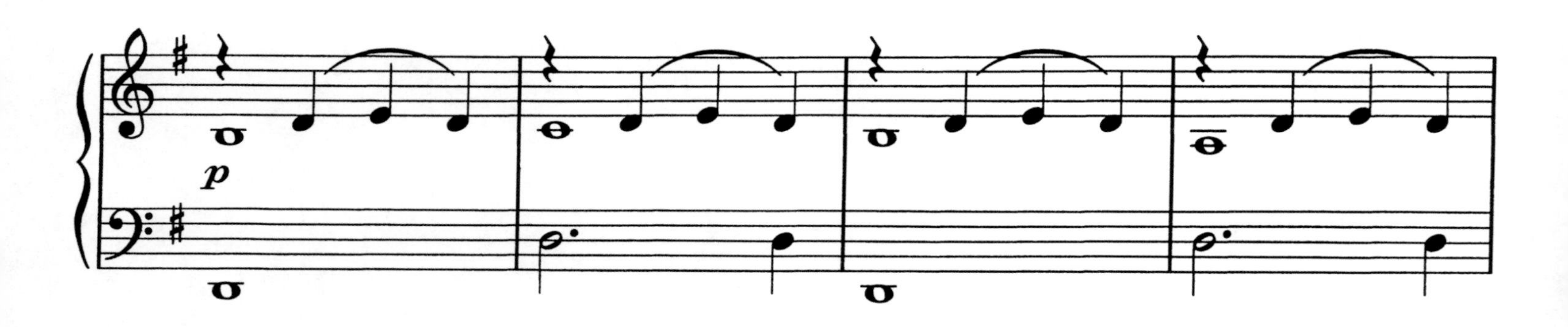

The Wild West

Student

Boldly *One octave higher with duet*

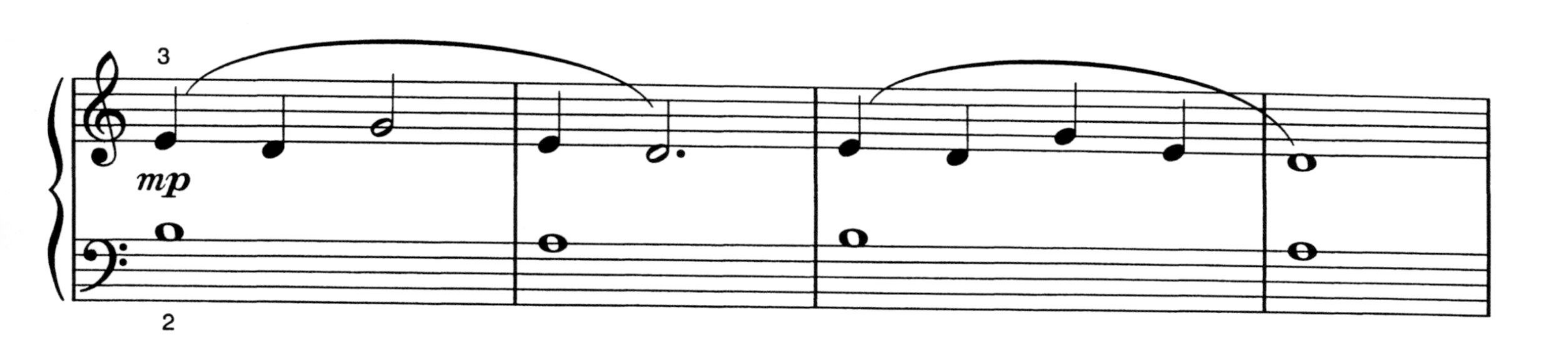

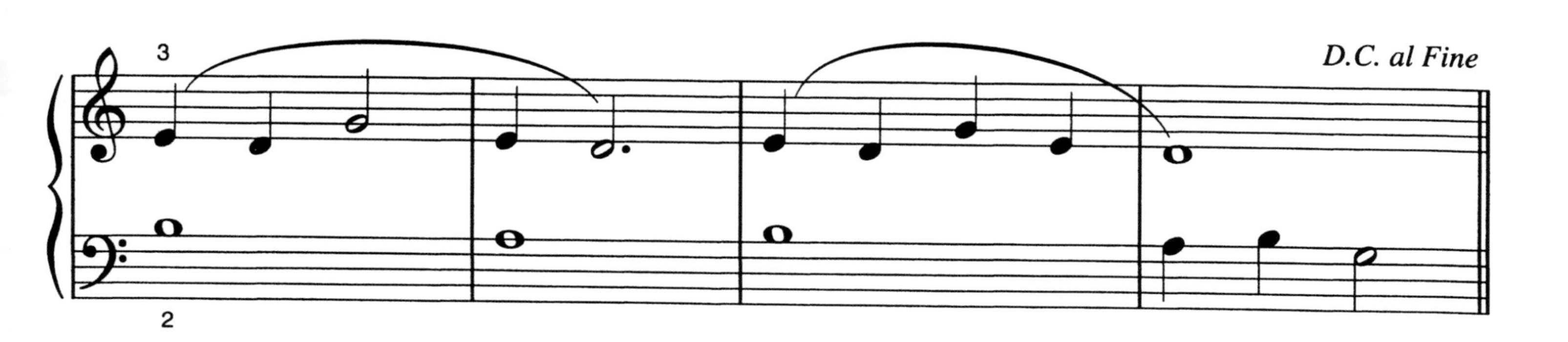

A Gentle Breeze

Teacher

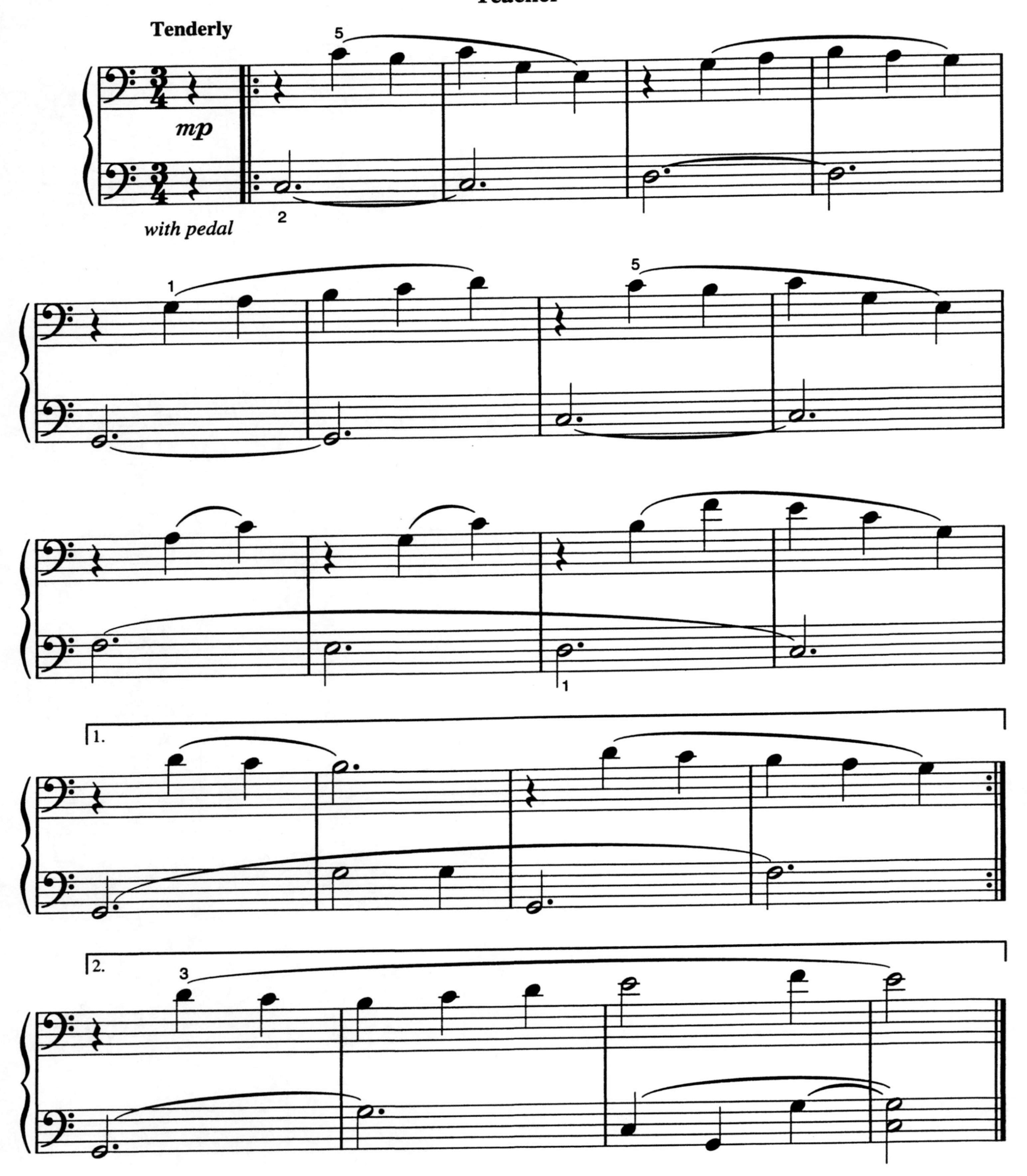

A Gentle Breeze

Student

Inside the Pyramid

Student

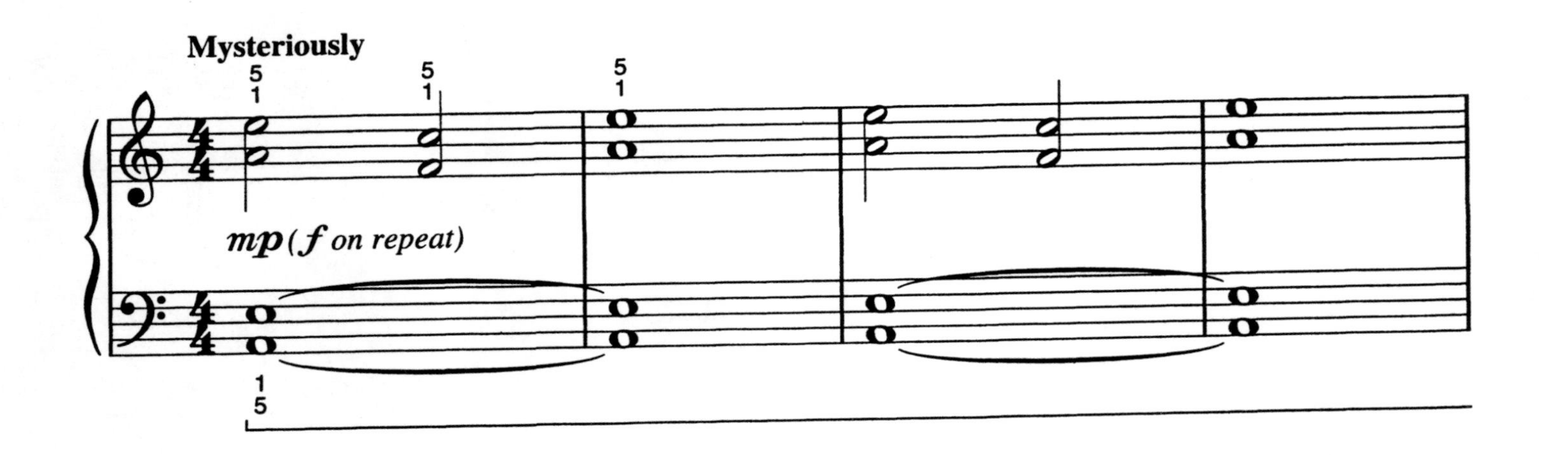

Inside the Pyramid

Teacher

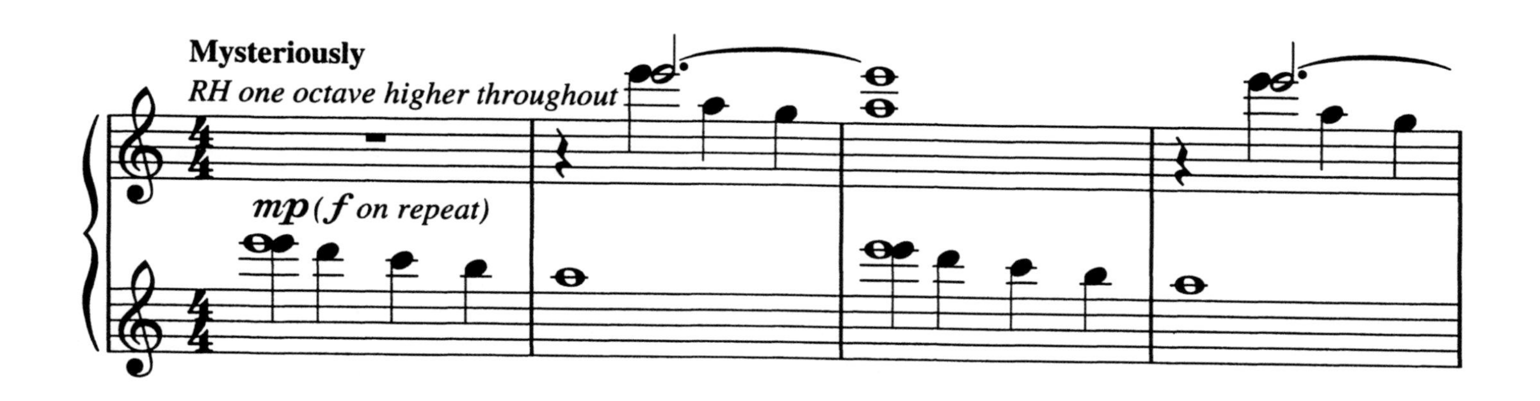

The Matador

Student

The Matador

Teacher

Brother John

Student

Traditional

Brother John

Teacher

Traditional

Rodeo

With energy **Student**

Rodeo

Teacher

With energy
Introduction

Above the Clouds

Teacher

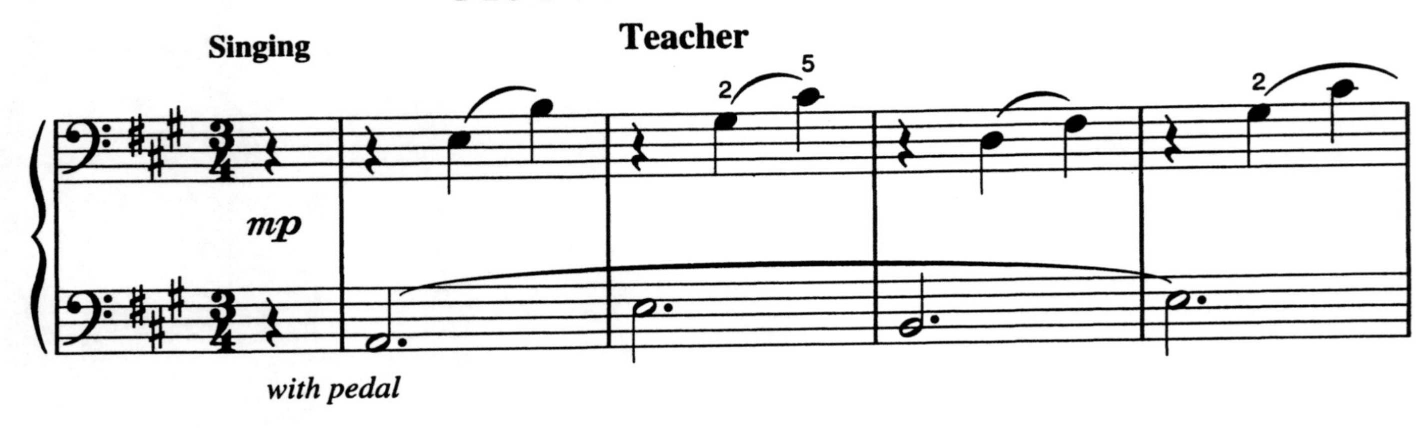

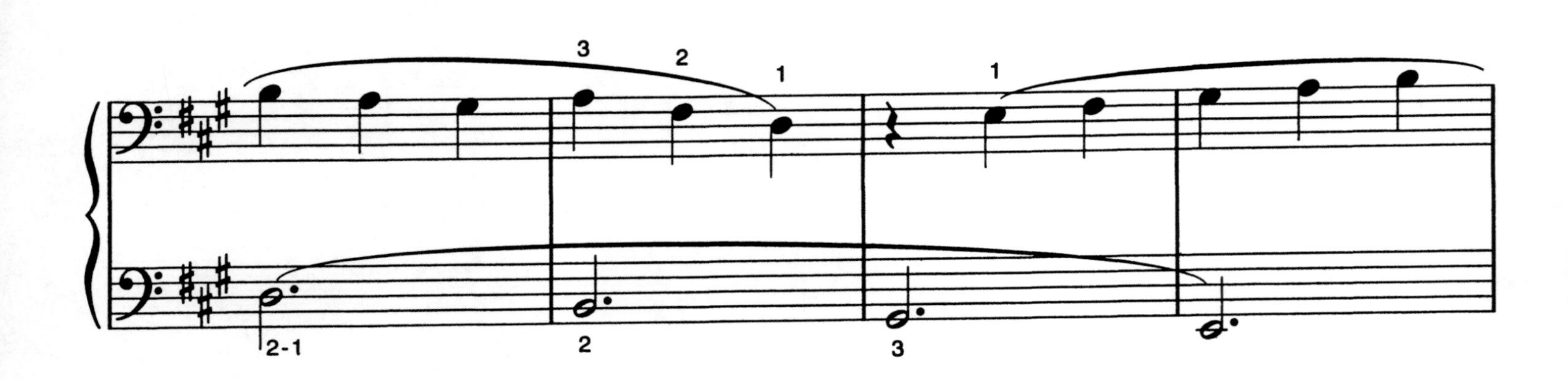

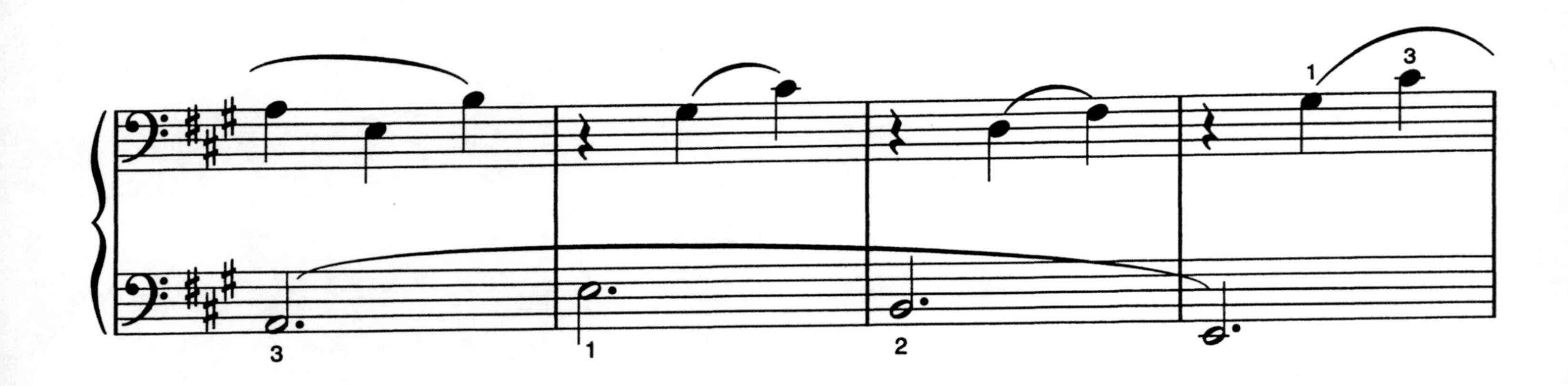

Above the Clouds

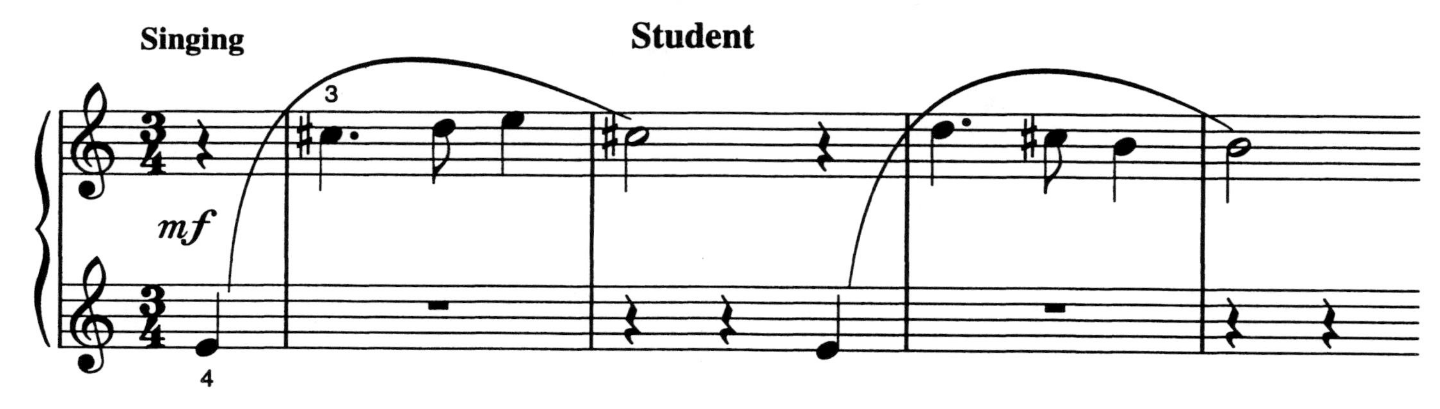

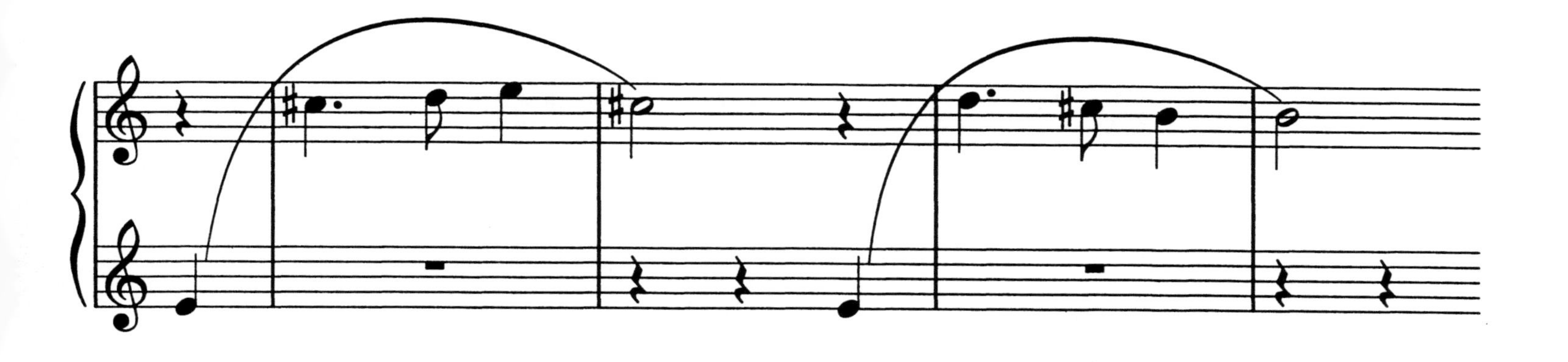

Cathedral Bells

Teacher

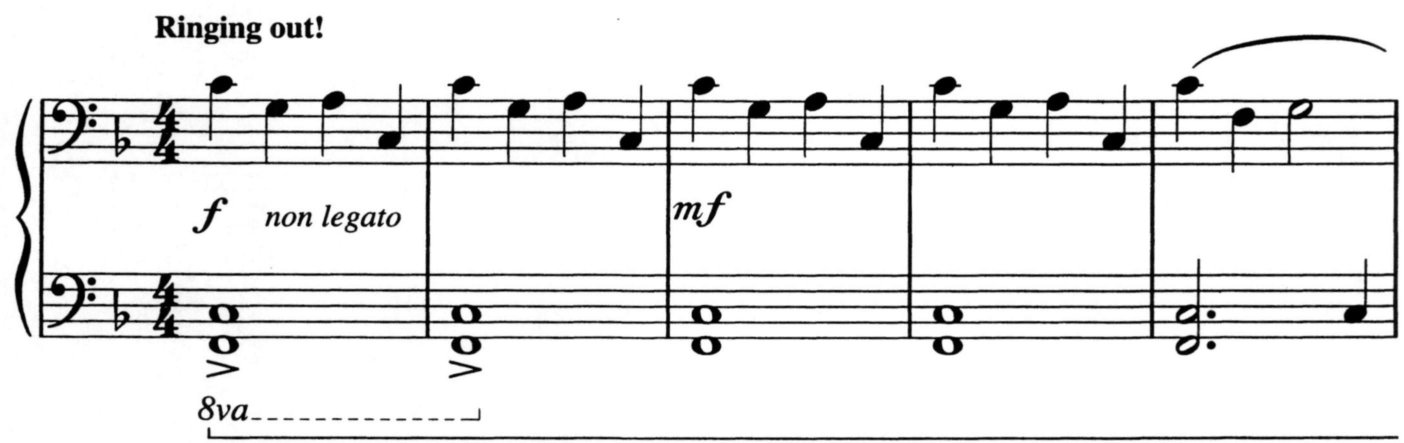

0689

Cathedral Bells

Student

Ringing out!

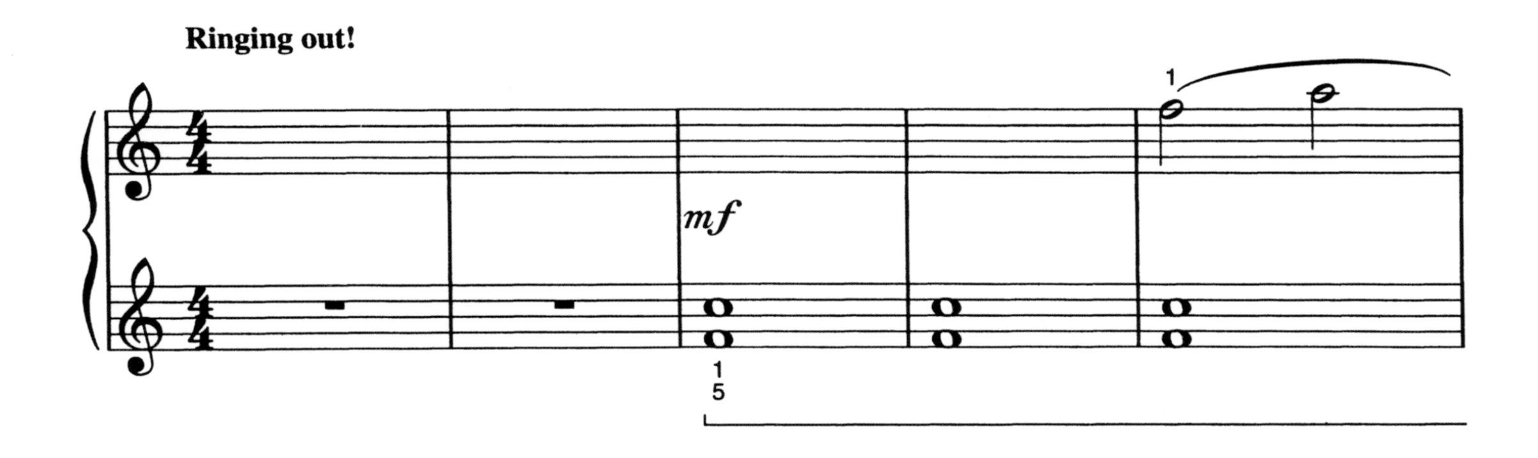

Scarborough Fair

Teacher

Scarborough Fair

Student

Sadly

Traditional

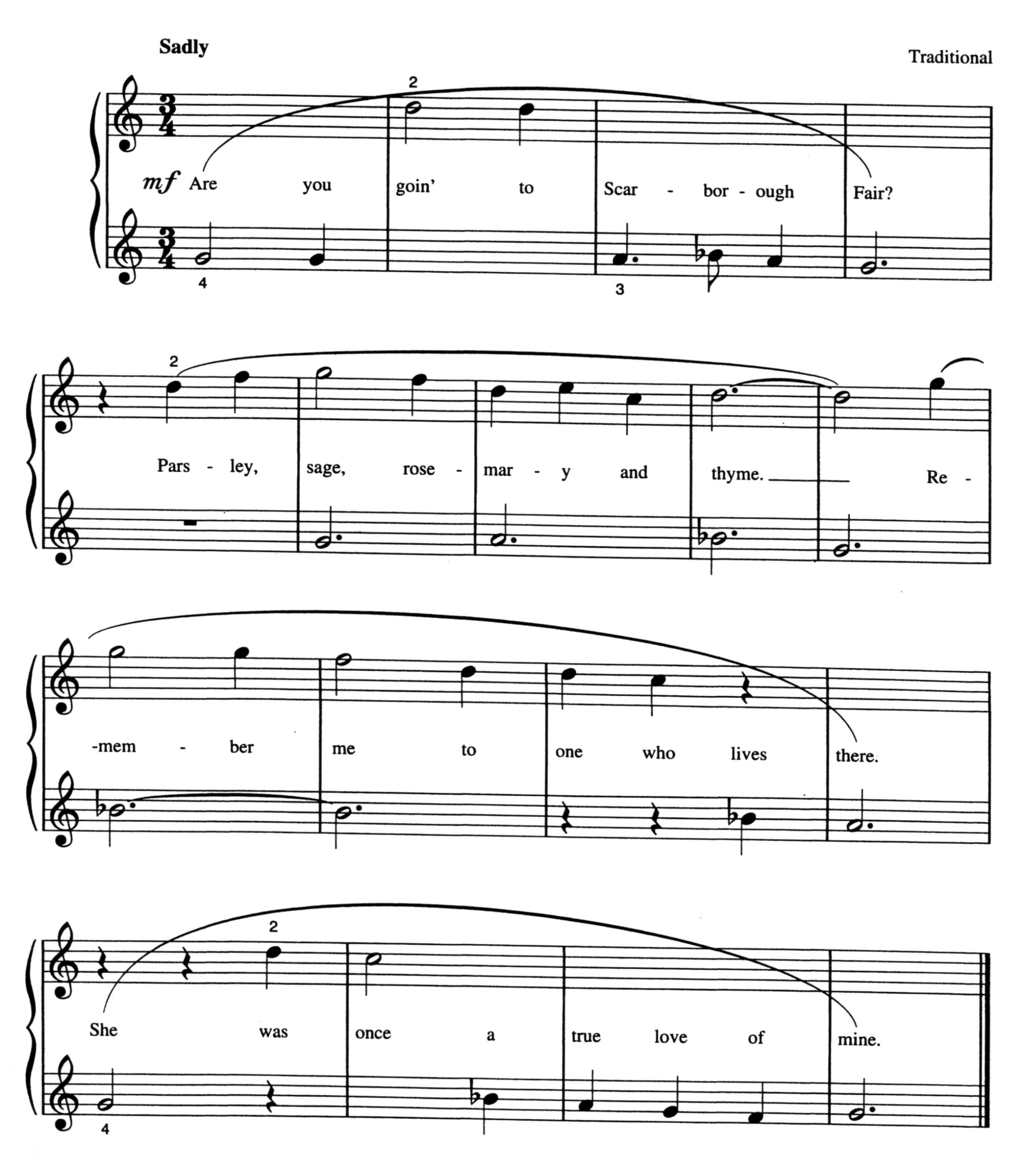

Snowy Day

Student

Snowy Day

Teacher

Homework Blues

Student

Homework Blues

Teacher

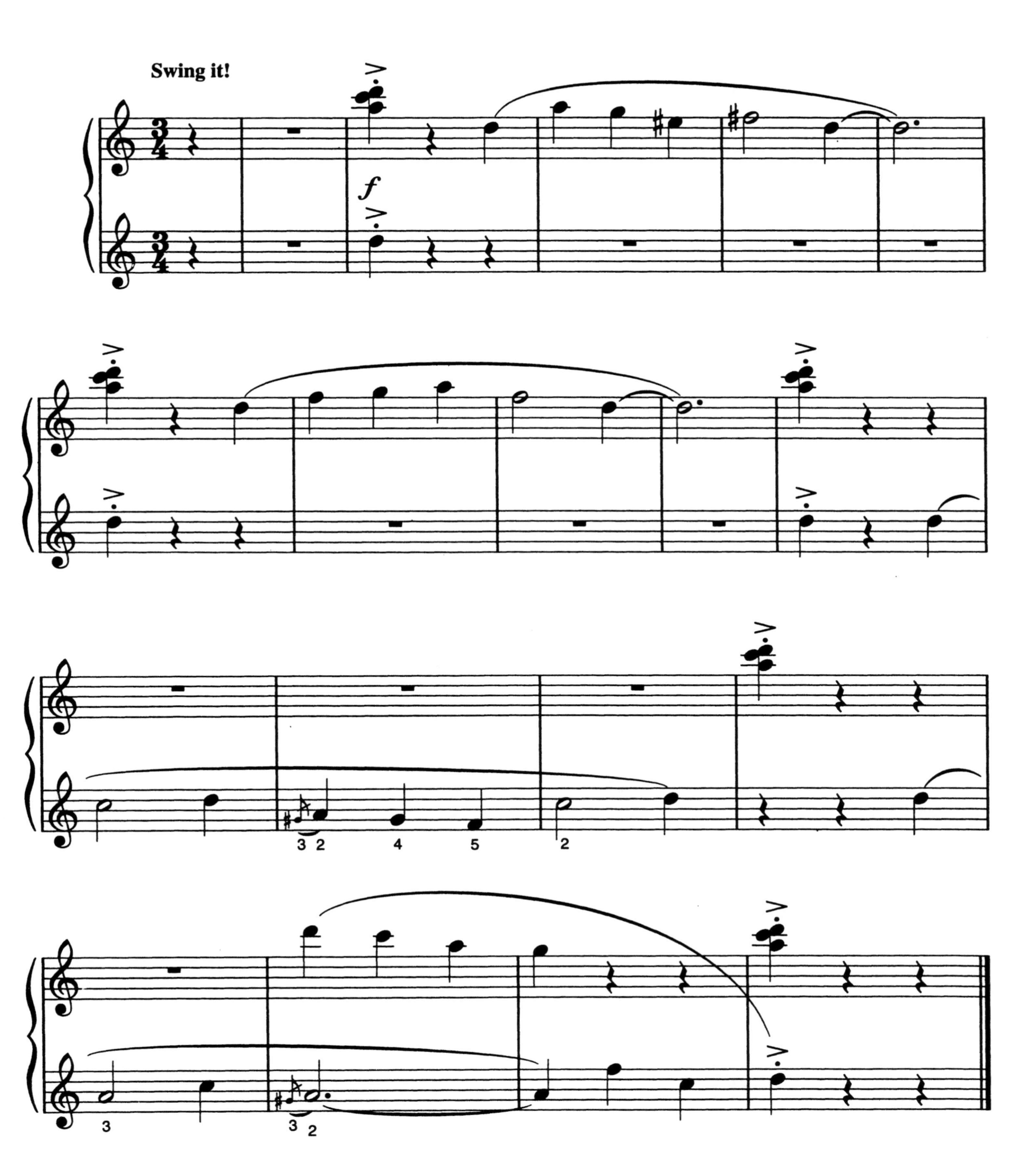

All the World Is Sleeping

Student

All the World Is Sleeping

Teacher